Acknowledgements

Thank you to Ira Pinkham and Bryan Kelley
for sharing your memory of a day on the ocean.

Sun-up in Five Islands,
Ira and Bryan are goin' haulin',

boots on,
and oilskins.

"Pitch out some bait, Bryan,

I'll get the skiff," says Ira.

"Grab a bucket!"

"Goodbye, Five Islands!"

Hauling: pulling up lobster traps

Oilskins: waterproof coveralls

Skiff: small boat

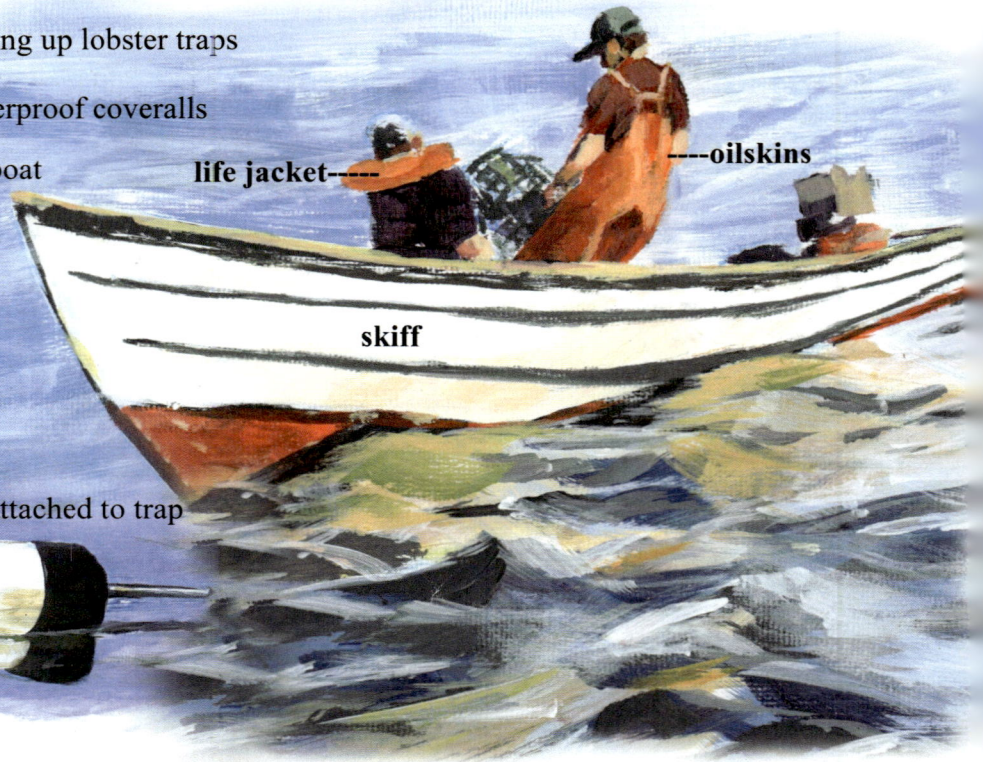

life jacket----- -----oilskins

skiff

Buoy: floating marker attached to trap

buoy

trap warp

Trap warp: line from buoy to trap

gaff hook

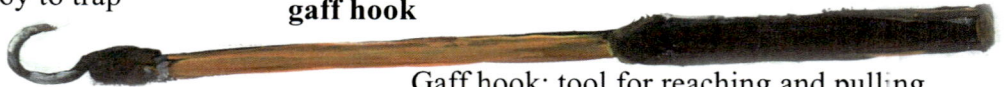

Gaff hook: tool for reaching and pulling

lobster pot or trap

bait bag

escape hatch

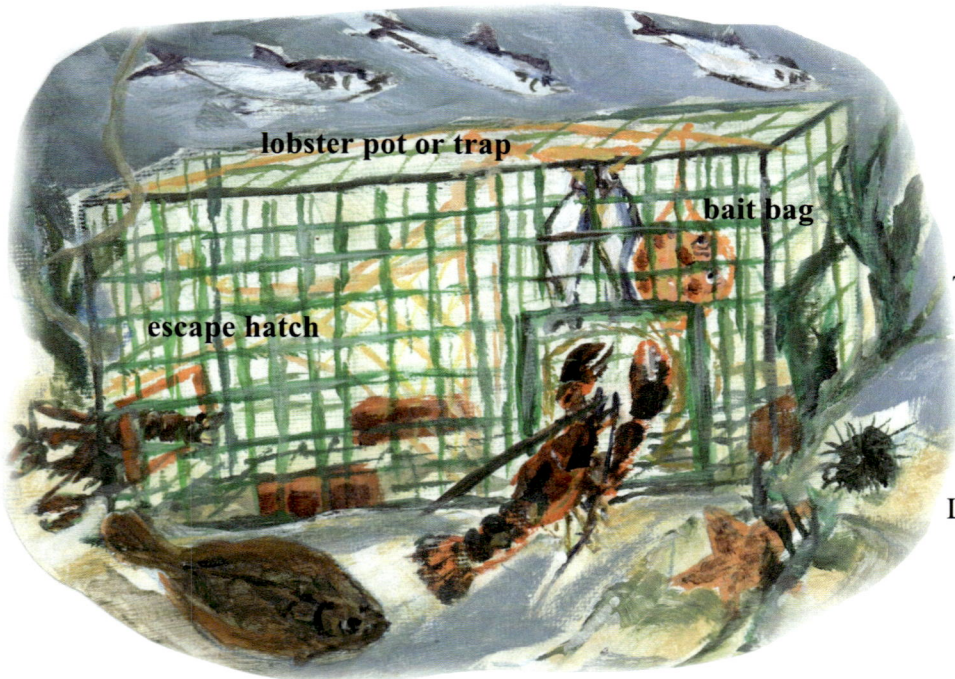

Lobster pot or trap:
Cage with bait
to catch lobsters on the
ocean bottom.

Trap has an escape hatch
to free little lobsters.

Lobster bait: fish that lobsters
like to eat.

We'll finish our work."

but first...

"Your friends are waiting for you,

"I'm hungry, Ira. What's in the cooler?"
"Never mind! I'll buy our lunch on the wharf."

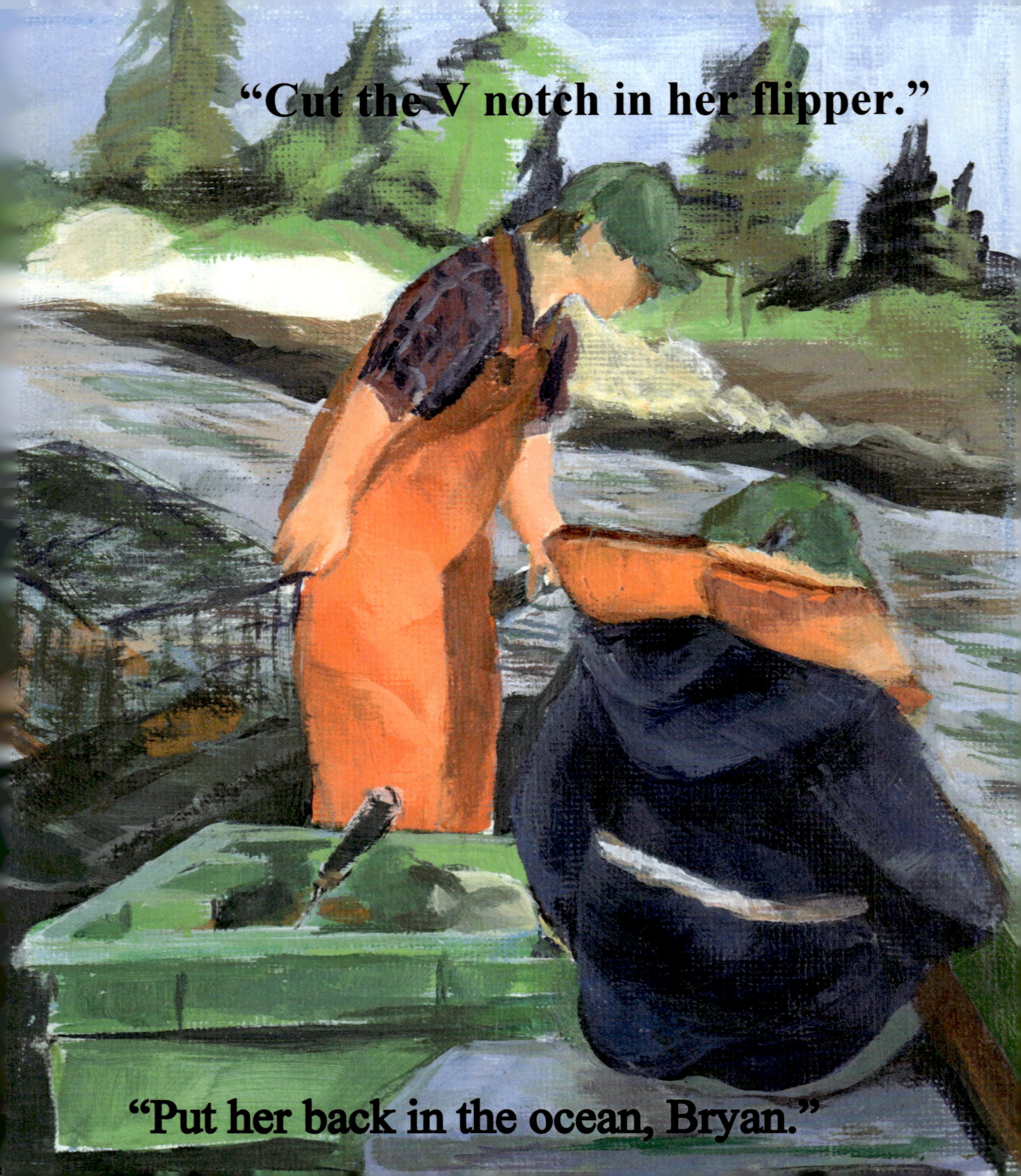

"Cut the V notch in her flipper."

"Put her back in the ocean, Bryan."

"Here's an egger!"

"Ah! The sweet smell of redfish and herring!
Just like candy! Right, Ira?"

"We need a good spot for this trap."

"Too short!"

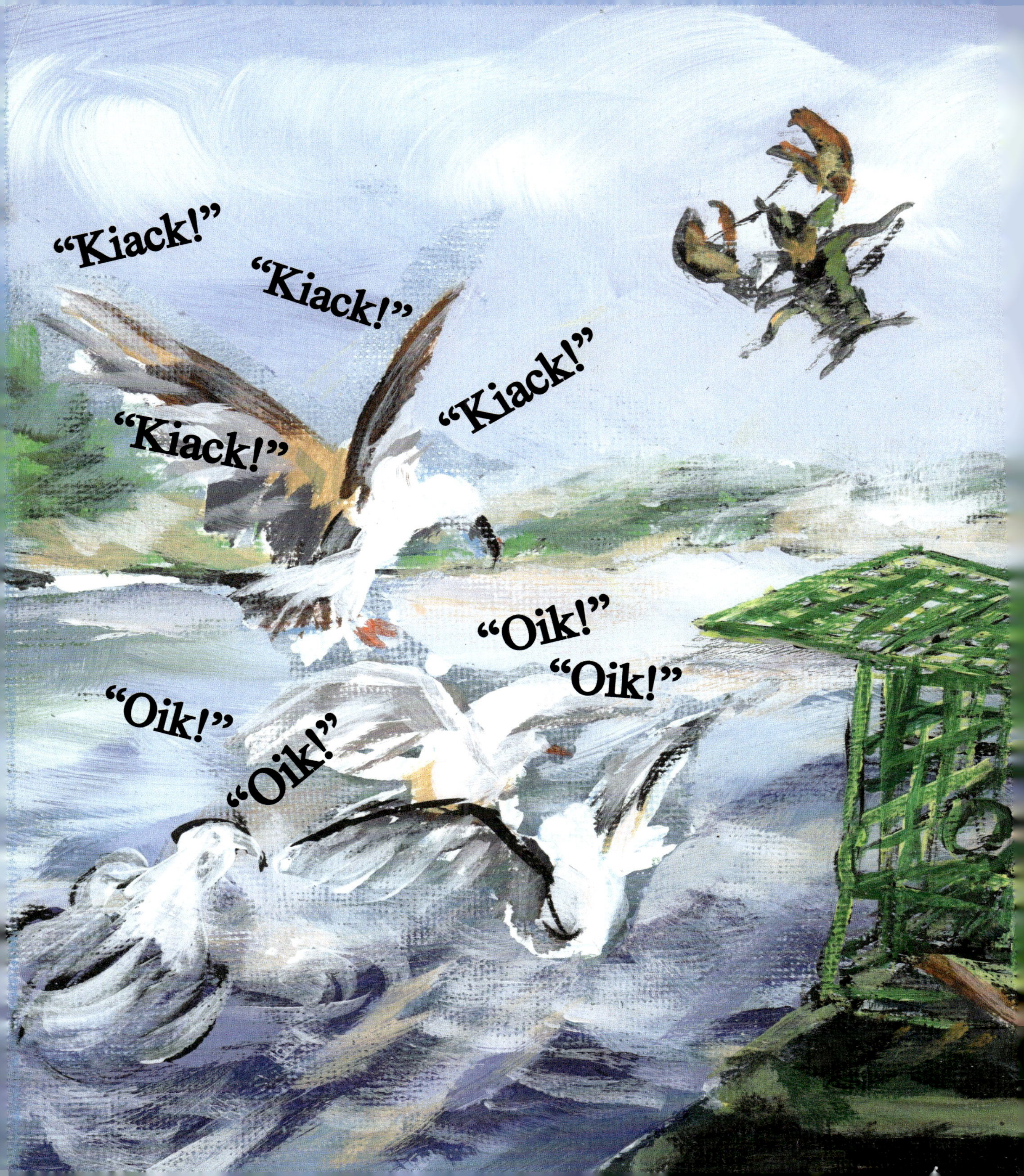
"Kiack!"
"Kiack!"
"Kiack!"
"Kiack!"
"Oik!"
"Oik!"
"Oik!"
"Oik!"

"I got it!"

"This one's a counter."

"Hand me the lobster bands, Bryan."

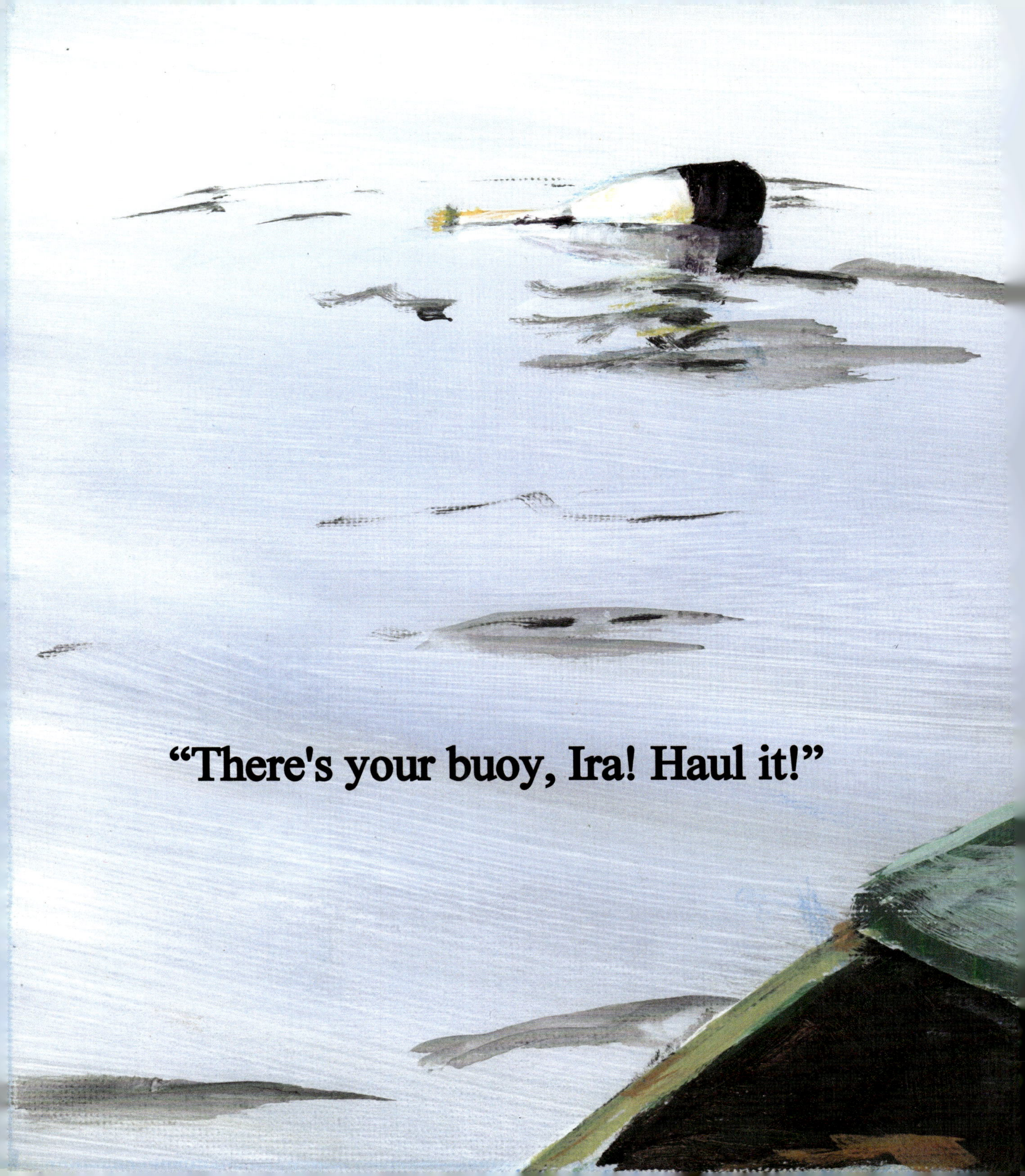

"There's your buoy, Ira! Haul it!"

Acadian Redfish

Sabastes Fasciatus

lobster bait

Atlantic Herring

Clupia Harengus

bait iron or needle

bait bag

"Counter" or "Keeper":
legal size male (cock) lobster
whose carapace measures
3 1/4 to 5 inches

Lobsters

Hemarus Americanus

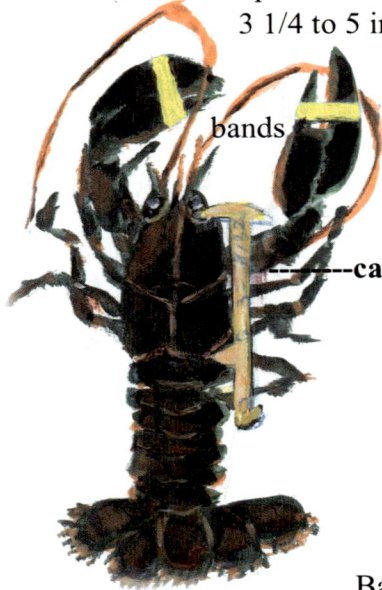

bands

Carapace: starts
behind the lobsters eye
and goes to the start
of the tail

‐‐‐‐‐**carapace gauge**

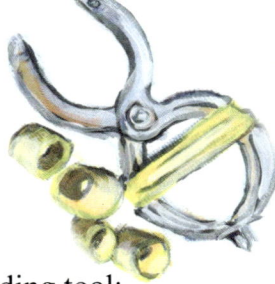

Banding tool:
puts rubber band on claws
to keep them from pinching

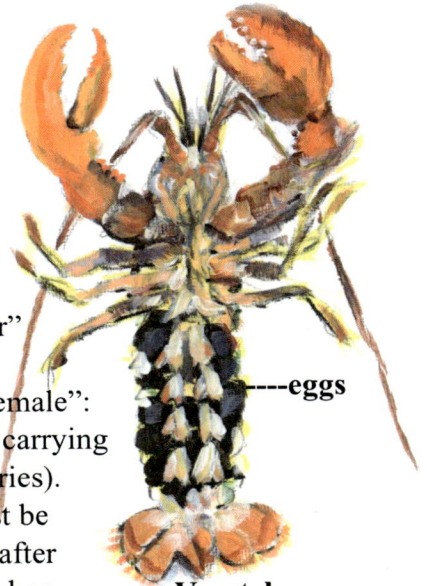

"Egger"
or
"Berried Female":
female (hen) carrying
eggs (berries).
She must be
released after
marking her
right middle
tail flipper
with a V notch
to identify her

‐‐‐‐**eggs**

V notch

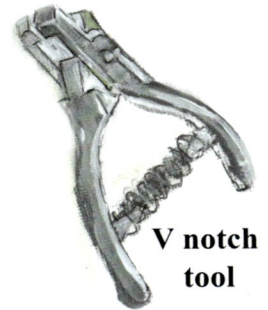

V notch tool

car

Car: floating crate
in which to store
live lobsters
at the dock